I'm pretty sure that animals can talk. They just don't want to ruin a good thing. We feed them and pet them and scooper their poopers. They repay us by lying in sun spots and napping. Animals are too smart to rock the boat. If they started talking we'd be obliged to invite them to staff meetings and put them on task forces and generally ruin their idyllic lives. If I were a talking animal I wouldn't say a thing. That's for sure.

Suppose the animals did decide to talk to us. Would they be courteous and polite? Would they care deeply about our opinions? I think not. They've seen us naked, so it's unlikely they have any respect for us. It's more likely they would treat us the way Dogbert does—as clumps of annoying organic mass that provide occasional entertainment.

That's what this book is about. It's a glimpse into the personality of one talkative dog and the man he chooses to keep around the house. If you were wishing the animals in your life talked, this book will cure you. And when you have your health, you have everything—except for this book. So buy it and make your life complete.

S. Adams

ISBN: 0-8362-2197-4

CONVERSATIONS
WITH
DOGBERT™

A DILBERT™ BOOK
BY
SCOTT ADAMS

Andrews and McMeel
A UNIVERSAL PRESS SYNDICATE COMPANY
KANSAS CITY

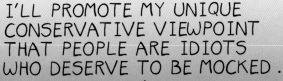

I'LL PROMOTE MY UNIQUE CONSERVATIVE VIEWPOINT THAT PEOPLE ARE IDIOTS WHO DESERVE TO BE MOCKED.

WON'T PEOPLE SHOW YOUR VIEWPOINT TO BE FLAWED BY VIRTUE OF THEIR INTELLIGENT QUESTIONS?

LIKE THAT ONE?

OUR NEW DRESS POLICY AT WORK ALLOWS CASUAL CLOTHES ON FRIDAYS.

ON THE CASUAL DAY DILEMMA

THE DEHUMANIZATION OF MY JOB HAS RENDERED ME INVISIBLE TO HUMANS. ONLY YOU CAN SEE ME, DOGBERT.

I DECLARE MYSELF THE PATRON SAINT OF TECHNOLOGY.

ON
SPIRITUALITY

I GOT A JOB AS THE HEAD OF MARKET RESEARCH AT YOUR COMPANY. I'LL BE PULLING DOWN $120K PER YEAR.

... ON HONESTY

TOMORROW I'LL SPEND THE ENTIRE DAY EXPLAINING WHY I DIDN'T FINISH YESTERDAY'S WORK.

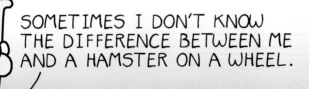

SOMETIMES I DON'T KNOW THE DIFFERENCE BETWEEN ME AND A HAMSTER ON A WHEEL.

HAMSTERS DON'T DEPRESS ME.

THIS SHOW IS GARBAGE.
I WILL ESCHEW IT.

CLICK

... ON
PERSONAL
HYGIENE